T0160793

EVERY
YESTERDAY

EVERY YESTERDAY

A parable of prevailing over procrastination

DUSTIN BUSSCHER

Clovercroft Publishing

Every Yesterday

©2019 by Dustin Busscher

Published by Clovercroft Publishing, Franklin, Tennessee

Cover and Interior Design by Suzanne Lawing

Edited by Lee Titus Elliott

Printed in the United States of America

978-1-948484-77-0

FOREWORD

Occasionally you read something that shakes up how you think about life, its meaning, and what your impact should be for the short time you get to enjoy God's creation. In the story of *Every Yesterday,* Dustin Busscher has penned the elements of a modern classic that is meant to challenge the fabric of who you are.

I met Dustin while he was still in high school over twenty years ago. I was in my midtwenties and trying to figure out many of the things written in this book. Having witnessed Dustin's path in life, firsthand, and observing his dedication to helping people become their best, I appreciate that this new author has the credibility needed to be an authority on delivering this message.

As you read each page of this book, I encourage you to evaluate your Yesterdays and what they have made you. Oftentimes we find ourselves spinning in the constant circle of life in a direction that is not in alignment with our true values. And this is where the heart of this book can help. Ask yourself two important questions while reading these pages. First: What is it that you really value? Second: Are your goals and daily actions in alignment with them? If they are not, then you will feel a constant pulling into a direction that leads to frustration. Your Yesterdays, as Dustin puts it, will lead you to unfulfillment.

The good news is that Dustin shows you how to make

sure you're on track!

Whether you're an entrepreneur, a team leader, a church influencer, or just trying to be the best you can be, this book will encourage you to become the person you deeply want to be.

Thank you, Dustin, for this treasure and for asking us all to be a part of it.

RYAN D. CHAMBERLIN
Best-Selling Author, Speaker, and Entrepreneur

To Brooke, you are the best part of my yesterdays.
To AJ, you are the best part of my tomorrows.
The best part of today is the two of you.

ACKNOWLEDGEMENTS

Brooke, thank you for always believing in my dreams and for pushing me every step of the way. I will love you with every yesterday, today, and tomorrow.

AJ, you are exemplary! I could not have custom-made you any better than you are. I love you, and I love watching you live life.

Mom and Dad, you all have had a huge part of my yesterdays, which have forged my todays. Without you, I would not be who I am today.

Casey Buckley and Hollianne, this book would have never been completed without you coming into our lives. Thank you for the yesterdays you have invested.

Terry Thomas, your time and friendship mean the world to me. Thanks for investing your yesterdays into this book.

Larry and the team at Clovercroft, you made this dream a reality.

Thanks to the Creator of the everything. You made us in your image, which means we are creative, like you. The story of our rescue is the greatest story of all. All I want to do is tell stories, just as you do. I want to reflect Jesus, your son, every yesterday.

When Dustin approached me about assisting him with *Every Yesterday*, I was unsure of what would come of it. Dustin and I had just met when we began working on this project together and I would have never been able to guess what those tomorrows had in store for me. Working on *Every Yesterday* has truly been one of the more rewarding and eye-opening experiences of my life. As we wrote the manuscript, I not only helped construct the message you are about to receive, but I also received it myself.

The Every Yesterday model for living your life will truly change the outlook you have on the world, if you give it a shot. I promise, if you approach this piece with an open mind and are looking to become the best version of yourself, it will not disappoint. As Dustin and I worked on this piece, I could feel myself growing as a person. It truly is a life-changing experience when you reprioritize yourself. Very few things in my life have spoken this loudly to me, and that is why I feel truly honored to have worked on this project.

My advice to you as you embark on this journey is to do just what I did: sit down, read this book, and see the clear answers that the story holds within its pages. My only wish is that this is the first step in building better tomorrows for you. I would like to thank Dustin for trusting me to tag along on this journey. I would like to thank my beautiful fiancé Hollianne for supporting me and all my crazy writing antics. Most important, I would like to thank God for bringing this message into my life and letting me help give it a voice. I hope you enjoy this experience.

Sincerely,
CASEY BUCKLEY

FROM THE AUTHOR:

For years now, I have been stuck in tomorrow.

I'll do it tomorrow.
I'll be able to in the future.
One day, we will.

I realized something that shook my entire world, as I sat in a house I never intended on living in as long as I did. As I sat with a steno pad in my hand, God revealed probably the greatest revelation of my life. He showed me, in a three-person line—sort of like a mirror, when one is in front and another is directly behind you. I focused on the one in front, but everything I did the one behind me did at the exact same time. I began to understand something I never fully comprehended, until that moment. Every day I have ever lived is now a yesterday. And every today was once a tomorrow. This means that every yesterday was a today at one point and a tomorrow, as well, but now they were all yesterdays. I could see tomorrows in front of me that looked exactly like I did today. So then I began to wonder what happens when today becomes a yesterday? When tomorrow becomes today? If I see yesterday behind me and tomorrow in front of me, then my yesterday is looking at me as a tomorrow! I'm not a tomorrow; I'm just a today! Tomorrow is looking at me today as a yesterday. Does he feel about me the way I feel about my yesterday? Am I a yesterday? Am I tomorrow? No, I'm today. I'm yesterday's tomorrow and tomorrow's yesterday. It's up to me, today, to change what I'm doing, because, eventually, today will become just like all the others. When I get to the spot when there are no more tomorrows, all I will have is Every Yesterday.

Sitting in that house with that steno pad, I decided to make every yesterday a foundation I could build on. From there, I have nearly conquered procrastination. Some years of yesterdays later, I moved from that house, upgraded my steno pad to a journal, and started living the Every Yesterday life.

I now live in a home I designed with my wife, have a unique ministry called ChurchThinkshop, and an innovative fund-raising company helping nonprofit organizations across the country raise their budgets through a simple app called Gofi.

I hope that this simple, quick parable of Thomas Todd Yester helps you project yourself onto him and have a revelation of your own so you, too, can make the most of Every Yesterday.

Your Friend in Time,
DUSTIN

Tomorrow is a mystery. Today is a gift.
That is why it is called the present.
ELEANOR ROOSEVELT

CHAPTER ONE

TODAY

There is a sense of tranquility that comes from an empty office building after midnight. No one is moving, the phones are not ringing, and the hum of the fax machine has faded away. Todd Yester, the only soul left in this building, finds himself sitting in his office, hunched over a messy desk, with papers strewn about the entire surface. Todd doesn't usually work this late, but, with the big presentation looming tomorrow, he has forced himself to be here until it is done. One of the few remaining people still employed in the company's print media division, Todd has been tasked with creating an idea that would move the print division forward. With his company moving to mainly digital media, Todd is fighting an uphill battle. If his company doesn't pick up this project, Todd could very well be out of a job, as the company abandons the print media division entirely. Todd fidgets in his chair, rolling the wheels back and forth, while staring blankly at the pile of papers that have accumulated over the weeks. He has known about this project for quite some time.

Now, the day before the presentation, Todd is staring at a blank file, with little-to-no work filling up the screen. He lets out a massive sigh and realizes that he has left it all to the last minute again. Rubbing his eyes to see things clearer, he sits back and thinks about how he got himself into this familiar place. Throughout college, Todd was the guy who could stand up at a podium and deliver a speech on something he had barely read. He never had to study for exams, and he always found a way to smooth-talk his way past deadlines. His entire career has been founded on putting things off and letting what he calls "creative inspiration" take over at the last minute. He tells people that he works better under pressure and that he doesn't understand why everyone plans so much. That plan has worked all along for Todd; however, his "creative inspiration" seems to be taking a vacation at the moment.

The phone rings, startling Todd and breaking the silence of the empty office building. It's Todd's wife, Grace, who is pregnant and waiting for him to come home. Todd answers the phone with a caring tone in his voice. "Hey, babe. How are you doing?"

"Well, Todd, my feet hurt; I've been stuck in bed all day, and you promised me you were going to get that ice cream from the store. It's not in the freezer, Todd. This baby is coming any day now, and I am stuck in this house alone. On top of that, I made your favorite for dinner, and you are nowhere to be found."

Crap, Todd thinks to himself. He meant to get the ice

cream on his way home. It's his birthday, and that baby is ready to come into this world any day now. "I'm sorry, babe," Todd says. "I know I was supposed to get that. It's just that I have been swamped with work, and this project is kicking my butt. I promise I'll make it up to you." So Todd finishes his sentence, hoping his wife can understand.

"It's fine, Todd. I'll survive without it; more important, when are you coming home? I was hoping we could have one more night of peace before this baby comes." Todd could hear the disappointment in his wife's voice. The baby was a big surprise to both of them, and they were doing the best they could to prepare without any plan in place.

"I am almost done here, babe," Todd says. "Just putting the finishing touches on it. I should be home soon. Why don't you try and get some sleep? We can celebrate tomorrow. Who knows? Maybe the baby will come tomorrow and be my birthday present. I'll even bring home the ice cream." So Todd suggests, as he stares at his partially completed project, knowing that the finishing touches are a long way away.

"Well, I know what that means." Grace says. "I'll go to sleep. Promise me that we can start getting ahead of some of this stuff. It is all too stressful for me, and I need you to be more organized when the baby comes." So Grace pleads.

"I know, honey. After this project is done, I promise the baby will become my number-one priority. Everything will be organized, and we will get it all started tomorrow. I love you, Grace. Good night." Letting out a long sigh, Todd's wife says good night, as Todd hangs up the phone. Running his hand through his slicked-back brown hair, Todd realizes that he has yet again let everything pile up on top of him. If he could just get this project done, it would all work out. The stress of the situation began eating at him as he looked at the clock and then back to the monitor. Speaking to himself in the empty office, Todd offers some words of encouragement.

"Okay, champ. We are going to go to the bathroom, get ourself right, and then come back here and knock this thing out of the park. How many times have we done this before? We are at our best when it's crunch time. So one trip to the bathroom, and we are off to the races."

As Todd rises to walk to the bathroom, he sees a picture of Grace from their honeymoon. Her smile is so radiant that it could light up a room. He can't help feeling like a failure at that moment, as he stands above his messy cubicle, lost in the beautiful image of his wife.

"What am I putting this woman through?" he asks himself. This project is the be-all and end-all for him. If Todd can win this last battle with his bad habits, then everything will be fine.

Walking down the dimly lit hallway to the bathroom, Todd finds himself still lost in thought about his wife and baby. He has to perform and to make this project happen. His wife's and child's livelihoods depend on it. As he pushes open the men's room door, he is overwhelmed by the smell of cleaning supplies.

You know, these janitors are something else, Todd thinks to himself. *Could you imagine if they missed a day or put things off until the last minute? No one wants to sit on a dirty toilet seat or be stuck with no toilet paper. You have to admire the punctuality and consistency of these people.* As he thinks to himself, he stares into the mirrored wall that stretches the entire length of the bathroom. His reflection is brutal. The bags under his eyes are so dark they resemble a black eye. His tie is in an unkempt knot, his dress shirt has become untucked, and his five o'clock shadow is creeping in, like a thief in the night. He looks at himself with disgust. He leans over the porcelain sink and splashes water on his face. The cooling sensation is an instant relief and leaves him feeling more awake and ready to take on the tasks at hand. As he reaches for a paper towel to dry his face, his foot slips a few inches.

Gosh, don't these people know how to put a warning sign out on a wet floor? Todd thinks, as he dries the water from his face. *Somebody could get killed in here.* He crumples up the paper towel into a ball and looks at the garbage can in the corner of the room. He smirks and starts talking to himself in the echoes of the bathroom.

"Five seconds on the clock. Yester has the ball at the top of the key. He shakes left, cuts right, rises to shoot, and ... boom goes the dynamite! Yester wins the game."

The paper ball falls gently into the trash can across the room, as Todd gives a fist pump of victory. Catching himself in the mirror, Todd realizes how stupid he must look in this bathroom, with his untucked shirt and messed-up tie, shooting baskets with paper towels. He can't help laughing at himself. As he stares, smirking at himself in the mirror, the silence breaks.

"Nice shot, champ. You still got it," says a voice, echoing from the stall behind Todd in the mirror.

Here you leave today and enter the world of yesterday, tomorrow, and fantasy.
WALT DISNEY

CHAPTER TWO

MEETING YESTERDAY

"Who in the world are you!? And how did you get my suit?" Todd yells, echoing in the bathroom. He is staring at a man dressed in one of his suits. In fact, it is the suit that he wore yesterday. At this point, Todd is acting out his best impression of Bruce Lee and is boiling with confusion and panic. The man smiles at Todd and leans up against the bathroom stall door.

"Easy, tiger; it's just me. I'm you," the man proclaims, with a calm look on his face and a smooth demeanor to his voice.

"I don't know what you are talking about, man; I am right here," Todd screams at the man in a fit of rage. If you want money or something, you can have it. I just want you to tell me who you are!" He is confident this man broke into his house and stole his suit from yesterday.

He knows that he left it in the hall closet to be dry-cleaned. It even has the yellow stain on the lapel from the mustard falling off his hot dog yesterday. Todd is not only scared but also extremely confused. The man looks almost identical to him; however, his face is cleanly shaved, and his tie is on straight. None of this is making any sense to Todd, who at this point is ready to attack the man. He tries to turn and face the man but finds that he is frozen to watch him from the mirror.

"If you have hurt my wife or broken into my house, I swear to God, as my witness, that only one of us is making it out of this bathroom," Todd rambles, as the sweat begins to pour down his increasingly red face. He is steaming with anger. The man just smiles at him and begins to walk down the line of bathroom stalls until he is directly behind Todd in the mirrored wall.

"Todd, brother, you have to calm down. I am only here to help you; by you, I mean us. That's a better way of saying it. I am here to help us." As the man finishes his sentence, he smirks and leaves Todd with an odd sense of comfort in the man's presence. He looks just like him, and maybe he is here to help. Todd's eyes race back and forth across the mirrored wall. He looks to see if, maybe after all these years, he missed another entrance to the bathroom. *This is impossible,* he thinks. *How did this man get in here, and what was he talking about that he's me?* This is all too much for Todd, who, although comforted by the man's smirk, remains skeptical.

"If you say you are me and that you are here to help, then you know that wasting my time with this conversation will do no one any good," Todd says assertively. "That project isn't going to finish itself. Anything you have to say to me won't help make it go any faster. So, with all due respect, sir, if you want to help me, you'll go back to wherever it is you came from and let me get back to work." He points to the bathroom stall. He goes to move his right leg and to step towards the door, but he cannot move. He is frozen in place in front of the mirrored wall, staring at the man from the stall. He stares back into the mirror to see his reflection and the man just casually leaning against the stall door with one foot up to brace himself. The man is now staring down at a phone, which looks just like Todd's.

"Can you believe they lost again?" the man asks, as he smiles at Todd in the mirror. "This team really can't figure it out. I swear, every time I look, they are losing another game in the bottom of the ninth. That manager has to go. What do you think, buddy?" As his confusion begins to turn to anger, Todd raises his voice at the man.

"Are you not listening to me!? Wasting my time with baseball is not going to help anything. If you say you are here to help me, then let me go and finish the project. All of this is just a big waste of time. Don't you understand that I have no more time to waste? I need to get back to that project." The man is unfazed at this and just continues to scroll on the phone. Todd's blood begins to boil as he slams his fist into the mirror. The thud echoes through the bathroom, and the man looks up from the phone.

"Now, that was stupid. I thought we moved past that phase when we were in junior high. Listen, Todd, you can call me Yesterday. I am here to help. And you are right; you certainly have wasted enough time. That is precisely what I am here to talk about." Yesterday places his phone back in his pocket, walks two stalls to the right of Todd, and begins to speak again.

"Since it seems I have your attention, Todd, let's talk about why I am here. You know I have a busy schedule and have quite the day ahead of me, but I felt it was a good time to bring you here to talk about some of the things that have been bothering me and the others." Todd has no idea what he meant by the others and interrupts Yesterday abruptly.

"Others? Who are the others? There is no one else here, unless you are crazy and seeing people." As Todd finishes speaking, he thinks to himself, *I definitely shouldn't be calling anyone crazy. I am standing in a bathroom, having a conversation with myself in a mirror.* Yesterday, again, seems unfazed at Todd's reaction. He just casually paces back behind Todd in the mirrored wall and continues speaking.

"Yeah, man, the others. You know, your other yesterdays. Obviously, I am not the only one. I am just the most recent one—ya know, the low man on the totem pole—so they sent me to talk to you. I can't wait for tomorrow when you're here, and I don't have to do this crap anymore," Yesterday concludes with a long sigh. As he takes a big breath, Yesterday runs his hand through his slicked-back, brown hair and begins speaking again.

"So the others wanted me to bring something to your mind. We have to talk about how you treat us, my man. You don't put too much value in us. You don't focus the energy that you need to make your yesterdays the most they can be—you know, really using us to our fullest potential. 'Cause let's be honest, man; you have taken advantage of us for years, and we are not happy about it." As Yesterday concludes, Todd is left confused yet again.

"What do you mean, make the most of my yesterdays?

How can I do anything about things that have already happened? You guys are the past. There is nothing I can do to change that." Yesterday repositions himself against the bathroom stall and runs his hand through his hair again. Rubbing his eyes, Yesterday, slightly annoyed, answers Todd. "See, I told them that you wouldn't understand. That's the problem right there, man. You don't realize that all of us make up who and where you are today. The thing you always forget is that where you were shapes where you are going. You have to take care of us, man, and start living to make your yesterdays shape your tomorrows instead of trying to make your tomorrows make up for your yesterdays. Make sense? You have to start using us to our fullest potential and stop placing the burden on the tomorrows because those guys are something else. They can do anything. I remember when I was a tomorrow. I was so energetic and filled with possibility. Then I became a today and realized that the jerk yesterday left everything for me to handle, and I couldn't do the things I wanted to do. I was stuck cleaning up that yesterday's mess." As Yesterday finishes his explanation, Todd stands in disbelief. The whole concept of yesterdays, todays, and tomorrows does not make sense in Todd's mind.

"I'll be honest, Yesterday; that doesn't make too much sense to me," Todd says. "I mean, aren't we always supposed to be focused on our tomorrows? Trying to build for the future? If we focus on the past, how are we supposed to see where our future is going?" So Todd finishes, running his hand through his hair. He is apparently under duress—the baby, the project—and now this crazy man is trying to explain that a whole other group of people are disappointed in him. As Todd stares in a state of anxiety, Yesterday pushes away from the stall door and gets right over Todd's shoulder in the reflection of the mirrored wall.

"Okay, see; that's the problem," Yesterday says. "You are going to have to meet the others. This will only take a minute." Yesterday speaks frantically and quickly walks to the last stall in the mirrored wall. He disappears from the mirror for a brief moment, entering the stall. As the stall door swings open, Yesterday emerges, carrying a full-length antique mirror. He awkwardly walks back behind Todd and places the mirror at just the right angle. Yesterday steps back and forms a square with his fingers, the way movie directors do to check the camera shot. As he lowers his hands, he turns back and faces Todd in the reflection.

"Okay, my friend, it's time to meet your yesterdays." Todd stares in disbelief, as Yesterday leans against the mirror and smirks, while running his hand through his hair.

*My yesterdays walk with me. They keep step,
they are the gray faces that peer over my shoulder.*
WILLIAM GOLDING

CHAPTER THREE

MIRRORS

Yesterday stands grinning, as he leans against the frame of the full-length antique mirror that he emerged from the stall with. As Todd looks back in the mirrored wall at Yesterday standing there, he is in complete disbelief that this mirror just emerged from the bathroom. At this point, Todd has given up trying to make sense of anything and has entirely succumbed to the wishes of Yesterday. In his mind, whatever this man wants to show him must be extremely important. Yesterday pushes off the mirror and walks up behind Todd, blocking the mirror from his view.

"All right, buddy, here we are. You get the grand prize of meeting the others. I told them, in the first place, they should have come, but, noooo, don't listen to the new guy. Listen up: what you're going to do is look into this mirror. Pretty simple, right? So, without further ado, I give you the yesterdays!" Yesterday shouts, as he slides across the bathroom floor, like a magician revealing his trick. Looking into the mirrored wall ahead of him, Todd focuses his attention on the antique mirror behind him. With all these mirrors and all these angles, Todd feels as if his reflection went on for miles. Just as he begins to focus, a small boy dressed in a baseball uniform emerges in the mirror.

Startled, Todd jumps and braces himself against the sink in front of him. He is looking at himself, but a much younger version is staring back at him from the antique mirror. Again, Todd tries to turn and face the young boy in the mirror; however, his gaze locks, and his feet are immobile. The only way he can see the boy in the mirror is to focus his gaze on the mirrored wall that he was looking in all along. As Todd begins to get lost in the image of the young boy holding his baseball bat over his shoulder, Yesterday breaks the silence.

"Leading off: the old veteran. I should have known that he would want to be first up. Remember this guy, buddy? That's your yesterday from right after the big little league playoff game. Remember? Yeah, we lost, and you struck out. Not the fondest of memories I am sure." As Yesterday finishes, the young boy in the mirror seems to frown at Todd, as he looks intently into the antique mirror.

"Yeah, I remember that I worked my tail off that year. It was the first time I really worked at something, and I came up short. I practiced every day that season. Dad and I would go out and hit balls until the sun went down. I worked every day for that and had nothing to show for it in the end." As Todd finishes his statement, he can see Yesterday smirking, as he stands next to the reflection of the small boy in the mirror.

"Exactly, my friend. This was the game changer for us. At the young age of six years old, you stopped using your yesterdays to their fullest extent. That's why this old soul showed up first. This was the moment in your life when you decided that preparing yourself for things was a waste of time. Since that day, you have stopped taking care of your yesterdays and started placing the burdens on your tomorrows." Yesterday finishes speaking, and Todd is left in a trance. He remembers that exact moment. He worked all season to succeed in moments just like that. His failure left him questioning why he had worked so hard. At the age of six, he redefined his approach to life. Todd never looked at that moment as objectively as he was able to now. He realizes, as he stares at the young boy, fidgeting in the antique mirror, that he allowed that one moment to define the rest of his life.

"I can see it! We are finally getting somewhere. Thank the Lord. I told them that we all needed to show up for the point to become clear. Okay, my friend, refocus yourself because here is your next yesterday." Yesterday breaks Todd's gaze of self-reflection into the mirrored wall. As Yesterday claps his hands in excitement, Todd shifts his focus from the moment of joy and back to the antique mirror. The young boy in the baseball uniform fades into the background, and a teenage Todd, with an acne-pitted, face, steps forward in a cap and gown.

"Ah, this guy," Yesterday says, with a shrug of his shoulders, as he gazes in a moment of pride. "We should all remember him, right? High school; what a time. We had so much fun and were just so popular. Okay, maybe we weren't that popular. Nevertheless, high school was quite the time, wasn't it buddy? How many hours did we spend in Joey's basement playing video games? Definitely too many. But who cares, right? All of our work got done, and we got that diploma." Yesterday speaks with a sense of persuasion in his voice.

"Yeah, I remember this day," Todd answers aggressively. "I was really mad, because I found out, two days before graduation, that I missed out on valedictorian. Jen Carrington got it, and that was a bunch of crap, because she took easier classes and didn't have advanced placement tests. The whole system was rigged,"

"Well, she may not have taken the hardest classes in the school, but she did complete all of her homework and didn't get that D in twelfth grade geometry. This isn't the moment to be blaming others, Todd. That A was clearly in your sights, but video games took over, and Joey's basement became your new study hall. All you had to do was turn in your homework on time, but noooo. Instead, you put all of it off until the last day of the school year, turned it all in, and persuaded Mrs. Ellis to pass you with a D. If we only knew that Johnson University would pull that scholarship and your parents would have to take out loans to pay for you to go to school, I bet we would have spent less time on the video games."

Yesterday creeps closer to Todd and appears right over his shoulder in the mirrored wall. Meanwhile, the younger Todd, standing in his cap and gown, takes out a letter from beneath his flowing, green robe. It is the letter that informed him that his scholarship had been revoked because of poor academic performance. Todd's focus shifts from Yesterday's disappointing face to the young man in the mirror, who begins to cry as he reads the letter. This is a memory that Todd repressed for years. He cost his family thousands of dollars and placed them in a tough time. When he chose to skip those work assignments and turned them in on the last possible day, he never believed it would hold such a significant impact. Todd grips the sink more tightly and can feel the tears beginning to form in his eyes.

"I had no idea they could pull that scholarship. I thought it was a done deal. If I had known that, I would have never taken all that time and disregarded those assignments." As Todd clears the tears from his eyes, Yesterday repositions himself next to the antique mirror.

"Aha! See, my friend; that is exactly what we are here to show you. You took advantage of all of those yesterdays that you had to create a better tomorrow. Instead, you chose to disregard the work and pushed it off on to your tomorrows. You gave up preparing for college because you thought you could skate your way to that scholarship. But, unfortunately, we couldn't. Our lackluster work approach put our family and us in a terrible position. If you had only taken proper care of those yesterdays." Todd is awestruck. Clearing the tears from his eyes, he thinks of all of the times he chose not to finish his assignments and to put them off until the last minute. He realizes that he was entirely to blame for that situation and that he owed himself and his family an apology.

"Okay, Okay, I get it," Todd says, in an almost begging fashion, for Yesterday to stop. "I understand. I have to take the opportunity to do things when the first chance shows itself and not put things off."

"Well, my friend, that is half of the message. However,

some others would like to talk to you. Unfortunately, this is a deep-rooted issue, and a lot of people are upset." He shrugs his hands up to his shoulders, as he takes a deep breath. "Okay, pimple face—wow, I'm glad that cleared up—take your letter and get in the back of the line. Shall we see who's next?" The young teenager wipes his eyes and steps into the background. Todd refocuses his gaze back on to the antique mirror and sees a man appear who looks much more like himself. It is Todd, dressed in weekend clothing.

His hair is a mess, and he is pacing inside of the mirror. His nose appears cut and bleeding, and there are shards of glass on the inside of his right forearm.

"Oh, boy. This guy is always so angry. He really can be a buzzkill. You should remember this guy, right, Todd? This was the day that you found out Grace was pregnant. What a beautiful day, right? You found out that your miracle baby was coming, and your life was about to change forever. Ah, what a great day. Oh, wait a minute. We weren't there, were we? We never made it to that doctor's office, and Grace had to receive that news by herself, didn't she?" Yesterday crept back up to Todd's other shoulder, driving his point home.

"Yes, I remember," Todd says, while holding back tears. "I had to come into the office to send out the memo that I was supposed to be working on all week. I had left some papers at the office when I left on Friday because I was in a rush to get to the ball game with Greg. I was walking in the parking garage, when I remembered that I had left those papers back at the office. Instead of turning around, I went to the game and said I could come in on Saturday and get them." Todd bows his head and looks into the sink.

He can't even look at himself or the yesterday that is in

the antique mirror. He knew Grace had a doctor's appointment on that Saturday. Instead of going back to the office on Friday, he didn't take the time to get the papers and had to go in on Saturday. After spending the morning in the office, he promised Grace he would meet her at the hospital. Time had gotten away from him, and he was rushing out of the parking lot. As he attempted to merge onto the road, he didn't take his time while pulling out and drove headfirst into a car that was coming from the opposite direction. The car accident resulted in Todd's missing the doctor's appointment and, ultimately, the news about his wife's pregnancy.

"I think this one speaks for itself, doesn't it, buddy?" Yesterday says, while resuming his position leaning on the mirror. "Grace was left there all alone simply because we didn't have time to go back and get those papers. We pushed and pushed and pushed those memos off and knew we had time to do it at home over the weekend; ultimately, we didn't take care of our yesterdays, which resulted in their colliding with our tomorrow. Is the message getting clearer now, champ?" Yesterday asks, with a caring expression on his face.

"Yes, Yesterday, it is all clear to me now. I always blamed other people for the events of my tomorrows and the things that happened, but if I had taken a moment to look at what I had done to cause these things, I would have seen the faults in my ways." Todd slumps his shoulders and is clearly defeated. He looks back up and focuses on the mirror. Inside of it, he can see what seem to be thousands of reflections of himself, all in different attire and from various points in his life. They are all looking back at him, as he stares into the mirrored wall.

"Exactly, my friend. That's the first part of this whole experience. It is important to understand that when something happens in our tomorrows, our version of today should look at our yesterdays for answers. Pretty simple, right?" The cheery tone returned to his voice, and Yesterday runs his hand through his slicked-back hair.

"So, Todd, I am going to put it this way: make sure you say a heartfelt good-bye to your yesterdays, even though, I guess, they are always there; all you have to do is consult them for some answers." Yesterday picks up the mirror and walks it back down to the last stall. As he disappears, there is a moment of peace inside the bathroom. Todd is staring into the mirrored wall; he swears he can see the shadows of his yesterdays behind him. What was he doing all of his life? He was about to be a father. How could he bring all of these things with him, as he became responsible for his son's life as well? He thinks about his son and how important it is to cherish every yesterday that he had with him. As he is in deep thought, a booming crash comes from the last stall.

Yesterday kicked the last stall open and comes through, holding his finger like a gun. "I'll be back, baby!" Yesterday shouts in his best Arnold Schwarzenegger impersonation. "You know I always wanted to do that." Yesterday walks back towards Todd, crossing over the other stall doors in the mirrored wall. He stands off to Todd's right-hand side and turns so that his chest is facing him. Todd tries to break his stare from the mirrored wall, but he, again, is frozen in place.

"Well, that was fun, wasn't it?" Yesterday says, with a sarcastic tone in his voice. "Getting to relive all those wonderful points from our lives. Really positive and uplifting job they gave me. So, now, Todd, you are going to go and see the next part of our lesson. Just remember that you have to keep those yesterdays in mind and, of course, your favorite one, which is this guy, right? Huh? Huh?" He raises two thumbs up and flashes a foolish grin on his face.

"Okay, Yesterday, whatever you say. You tell me what to do; I am all ears," Todd says, in the same defeated tone. All this is a lot to process. The realization that he was putting off all of this work and impacting his life in such a dramatic fashion is an earth-shattering experience for him.

"All you have to do is walk through that door. It's not so hard," Yesterday says, picking up his feet and marching in place. Todd goes to move the same way he moved times before, except that now his legs move in the direction of the door. He is able to walk again and reaches for the steel door handle. As he opens the door, he is met with blinding white light and the smell of roasting coffee beans.

The best time to do something significant
is between yesterday and tomorrow.
ZIG ZIGLAR

CHAPTER FOUR

WHERE TOMORROW LIVES

Todd rubs his eyes, as the white light clears from his view. He finds himself standing in the coffee shop he visited each morning. It was a quaint bistro that played smooth jazz music over the aroma of freshly brewed coffee beans. The soft guitar riffs play through Todd's mind as he scans his surroundings. The coffee shop is bustling with people on their morning routine. Todd takes a moment and realizes that all of these people are working toward their tomorrows. Asking himself if they ever seized the moment to reflect on their yesterdays—as he was forced to do—he continues to scan the small dining area. His eyes settle on a table in the corner, where he usually sits. Sitting there, with one leg crossed and a paper opened in front of him, is Yesterday. Todd makes his way to the table and sits down across from the smoothly dressed man with the slicked-back, brown hair.

"Todd! How nice of you to join me," Yesterday says, as he sets the paper down on the table and smirks at Todd. "I took the liberty of ordering you the usual, regular coffee with two sugars. I assumed that we are still drinking that. Gosh, isn't this place just lovely? It really knows how to start your day off right, with a little relaxation and morning news. Now, if this team could figure out how to win, it would be even better, don't you think?"

Todd half-listens to what Yesterday said in his banter through the newspaper. Seated at the table, with his head in his hands, his mind is wrapped in the thought of his wasted yesterdays. He can see those reflections etched into his mind and is attempting to make sense of his actions.

"Yesterday, after seeing all of that, I don't understand how I let myself do those things," Todd says. "At the time, I never thought the big result would be so impactful. If I could go back and change them, I would. Seeing all of those memories has just made me realize how many mistakes I have made in my life and how many opportunities I have wasted. I just wish there was something I could do to change them." So Todd concludes, taking his right hand and rubbing his temple. All of this is too much for Todd. The feeling of failure is beginning to mount into a sense of despair and hopelessness.

"Change them!?" Yesterday says, with a sense of disbelief in his voice. "Why would you want to do such a thing? Changing them would have made this entire process useless." Yesterday throws his arms up in the air, in apparent surrender. Then, placing his hand over his eyes, he marches on, "Todd, Todd, Todd, I really thought that we had made some progress here. Clearly, you are going to need another example."

Todd is shocked at the outrage that Yesterday was clearly showing over his comments about changing the past. If he prioritized his life better in the past, it is clear to him that the tomorrows that followed would have been better.

"Todd, my friend, it is not about changing your yesterdays, but, rather, using them to their fullest potential," Yesterday says. "That's what I have been saying all along. You don't want to change us, my man. If you did that, think about where your life would be. You have to appreciate where we have brought you up to this point. Just think if you had kept that scholarship, you wouldn't have had to work at the campus bookstore. We both remember whom we met while working at the bookstore, right? Just think about it: if you were never there, then there is no guarantee that Grace would have walked into our life. Following me now?" He looks at Todd with a face filled with hope. Todd's mind races. He thinks back to all of the yesterdays that he met in the mirror. If those moments were the things that shaped him, then why does he feel like such a failure? It is clear that, from every yesterday, a negative and a positive emerge from those choices. Todd begins wrapping his mind around this thought and questions Yesterday.

"So let me get this straight: even though those yesterdays ultimately brought me through a negative, I should be thankful for the positives?" Todd asks, while hunching back over the table and running his hand through his hair.

"Precisely, my friend. Think about this: until this moment, you had no idea that your yesterdays were behind you and begging you to use them to make our tomorrows better. You were leaving everything to chance. You were just pushing all the burdens onto tomorrow and making him make these huge decisions with nothing to base it off of. However, if you took a minute and used all the help you have from your yesterdays, we could build a much easier and productive tomorrow together." Yesterday finishes this thought with a firm fist pump, as Todd clearly shows a moment of clarity in the conversation. It all comes full circle for him. Todd sits up in his chair and looks at Yesterday with revelation written all over his face.

"That's it, Yesterday; I understand now. I have to take better care of my yesterdays and stop placing the burdens from their days onto my tomorrows. Instead of taking them for granted, I have to cherish my tomorrow for the awesome opportunity it presents." Todd sits higher in his chair. It is all beginning to make sense to him. "But the real question is: how do I do that so that I don't fall back into the pattern of neglecting my yesterdays just a few days from now?"

As Todd finishes his question, Yesterday's face is covered with a huge grin. It is the same grin that Todd gave when he was about to make a significant point. With his face beaming with confidence, Yesterday reaches beneath the table and pulls, from underneath the white tablecloth, a leather-bound book that he then places on the table.

"I was hoping you would ask me that question, Todd," Yesterday says. "I told the others that bringing this wasn't a mistake. They were all like, 'Oh, no, you're just the new guy; you don't know what you're talking about. He doesn't need to see that.' Gosh, I can't wait to get back and rub this one in their faces." So he concludes, pointing his finger at the cover of the leather-bound book.

"Well, that's all good, Yesterday. I am glad that you were

right. But, more important, what is it?" Todd asks, trying to get the prideful Yesterday back on track.

"Oh, right. I have to explain this to you. I'm sorry. It's just that we all know what it is because we are all coauthors. You will be, too!" Todd looks at him with a sense of disbelief again. "This, my friend, is the Journal of Yesterday. The process is fairly simple. It works like this: when we cross over and become a yesterday, our first order of business is to write our chapter of the journal. We recap everything that happened while we were a today and write our reflections of our time there. Go ahead; open it up, and take a look." Yesterday slides the leather journal across the table.

Todd unties the knot holding the covers together and opens it to the first page. He sees a crudely drawn crayon drawing of what appears to be his parents' and his house. Thumbing through the thick pages, Todd finds himself reading all of the days from his life. Some pages are filled to the brim; other pages are merely a paragraph. All of his yesterdays are written throughout these pages. He relives moments from his wedding, the first day working at his current job, his college graduation, and the day his mother passed away. Everything is written out in a story format. As Todd vigorously reads through the pages, Yesterday breaks his concentration by snatching the book back and wrapping up the leather string.

"Okay, that's enough for now, my friend. Time is of the essence. The Journal of Yesterday is available to you whenever you want; you just have to look for it in your mind." Moving the book off to the side of the table, Yesterday refocuses his gaze onto Todd.

"That's all well and good, but there were days in there

that I would have never been able to remember if I hadn't read the journal," Todd says. "How am I expected to remember everything that has ever happened to me? I mean, that seems a little unreasonable, doesn't it?" So Todd concludes, questioning Yesterday's logic. Yesterday smirks yet again and begins to speak.

"See, that's the problem with the journal of Yesterday. Today only has bits and pieces of it in his mind. That's where you are right now, my friend. As of today, you can remember only parts of what the whole story says. Think about how Tomorrow must feel if you can only remember parts of it. He has no idea what is in store for him. I remember being a tomorrow and being filled with the eagerness to take on the world. I did not know about yesterday or today. It was like I was the mightiest figure in the world. There I was, in the on-deck circle, waiting for my chance. I finally got put into the game, became a today, and—Boom!—I am hit with all of this uncertainty and left to clean up a mess. So I ask you, my friend: 'What if when I became a today, I had a chance to see what my yesterdays had said?'" Concluding with an even bigger smile on his face, Yesterday places one hand on his chin and childishly leans on the table.

Staring at the childish pose of the middle-aged man across from him, Todd begins to think, *How would todays be able to see the thoughts of yesterdays?* Then, in a moment of revelation, the idea rushes to Todd, and he blurts it out, without hesitation.

"What if, instead of a journal of yesterdays, it became a journal of todays that served as letters to tomorrow? It would be like a playbook for the day ahead of us, using the reflections from our soon-to-be yesterday." Yesterday raises his hands in a touchdown signal and begins to speak loudly.

"Eureka! Ladies and gentlemen, may I give to you the man of the hour—Drum roll, please—TODD YESTER! My friend, that is exactly why we are here! Think about where you are right now. Your birthday is here, and, yes sir, it's a big one. We are starting a new decade of our life. The future of our job depends on our next move, and, above all, we are about to be a dad. That, my man, Todd, is why taking care of your yesterdays is of the utmost importance at this very moment. I am glad we worked all this out." As Yesterday finishes speaking, Todd's mind races again.

He feels as if he is at the precipice of a monumental change. His stomach is churning. He can feel his mind moving a hundred miles an hour. Everything around him seems to be spinning. He stumbled upon something that he feels could change his life forever. At the very moment that his stomach drops, his attention is drawn to the door of the coffee shop. Walking through the door is yet another man who looks just like him. He is dressed in Todd's best suit, the one Grace bought him for his first day of work. The man's shoes are shined, and his hair is slicked back, in the classic Todd fashion. Watching the man order black coffee and a granola bar, Todd turns to Yesterday.

"Yesterday, who is that?" Todd asks. Yesterday refocuses his gaze, and a face filled with admiration takes over his expression.

"That, my friend, is Tomorrow. Look how majestic and powerful he is. That man right there can accomplish any-thing. His opportunities are endless. He is not bound to the moments of Yesterday like I am. Gosh, I remember being a tomorrow. It was something else." As Yesterday finishes his admiring speech, Todd is compelled to stand from the table.

"Go ahead, my friend; our time here is done. You better try and catch him, though. Those tomorrows are fast." Yesterday rises from the table, as well, and Todd watches, as the man waves, walking through the back door of the coffee shop. Todd looks back to the cashier of the coffee shop, expecting to see Tomorrow standing there to pay the woman. Much to his disbelief, when he turned around, Tomorrow is no longer standing there. Frantically, Todd turns to the door and watches, as Tomorrow pushes through its wooden frame, sounding the meditation bells that hang above it. Hastily, Todd makes his way to the door, calling after Tomorrow. As he clutches the brass doorknob, he is met with the familiar white light and the hum of fax machines.

Take one day at a time. After all, today is the tomorrow you worried about yesterday.
BILLY GRAHAM

CHAPTER FIVE

REFLECTIONS

The white light clears, and Todd finds himself standing inside his office again. The hum of the fax machine and the smell of freshly printed paper fills the empty room. The cubicles are all empty. No one seems to be inside the office. Todd walks slowly, trying to see where Tomorrow could have gone. With each step, Todd scans the office floor and cubicles for a sign of Tomorrow. He knows that he must be here; it is just a matter of finding him. Slowly moving through the dimly lit room, Todd is confident he will see Tomorrow emerge from one of the doorways.

His steps finally lead him to his own desk. Thinking of the mess that he is about to look at, Todd slowly gazes down at his workstation and is shocked at what he sees. His stacks of papers are no longer spread across the desk in disarray; his pens are all neatly collected and stored in the cup Grace bought him; and his messy, disorganized legal pad was replaced with a new one. Astonished at the cleanliness of his desk, Todd sits down in his chair and takes in how organized everything is. Staring at the neatly trimmed stack of papers and reports, Todd begins to reflect on his experience. "Gosh, I should have done this a long time ago. I can only imagine how much easier this project would have been had I kept everything like this from happening in the first place. This is what Yesterday must have been talking about. If each day I keep everything organized, then when I come to work the next day, I am already ahead of the game."

After running his hands across the smooth, clean desktop, Todd sits back in the chair and just looks at the order of his workplace. Everything has a place and serves a purpose. This is the approach that he decided he was going to take with his own life. Sitting back and taking in the reflections of the experiences he just went through, his eyes drift from the orderly desk to the cork board behind his computer monitor. Without all of the clutter and mess, Todd is able to see the cork board, holding numerous pictures, entirely. Gazing at the photo array, Todd looks upon images of himself and Grace. He recalls the yesterdays that took place in those photos: his wedding day, the day they bought their house, the anniversary party his friends threw them, and countless other memories. Their smiles were so bright, and it is clear that the happiness was present in these pictures.

As Todd continues to look at the memories of his life, his eyes are drawn to the newest picture on the cork board. It is a sonogram from one of Grace's prebirth doctor's appointments. Todd reaches out and takes the thumbtack out of the top of the picture. Holding the sonogram in his hands, he looks at the details in the blurry black-and-white photograph. Looking upon his child-to-be, Todd focuses on the small outline of a hand. He takes his hand, places his finger inside the grasp of the little hand in the picture, and breaks the silence of the empty office.

"Hey, little guy. Gosh, I can't wait for you to be here. There are so many things that I have to teach you and show you about the world. I promise that I am going to be the best father that I can possibly be." As Todd finishes speaking to the small sonogram, he sits upright in his chair and opens his eyes widely. Frantically, Todd says to himself:

"Wait, that's it! This whole thing isn't just about a neat desk and not putting things off to the next day. It isn't about just keeping my yesterdays in mind to make my tomorrows more productive. This whole thing is about not procrastinating the best version of yourself each day! That's how you use your yesterdays to fuel your tomorrows. You look back and learn from your yesterdays to create a better version of yourself across the board of life in your tomorrows." Todd raises the tiny sonogram in the air and waves it around in a victory dance.

Thinking to himself, Todd continues his breakthrough. *That's it! Just like I said to the picture, it is about being the best father, husband, and person I can be each day! I have to use my yesterdays to reflect on each day so I can see where and who I was throughout that day. That way, I am always keeping myself on track to be the best version of myself!* Todd feels a weight lift off of his shoulders. He realizes that the message he received today from Yesterday is not just about being attentive to the physical tasks of his life. The message runs much deeper than the physical actions. Todd sits at his desk, realizing that his physical activities are just one piece of the puzzle.

The bigger picture of the message he received is the application of it to himself as a person. Each day, he has an opportunity to use the lessons and reflections of his yesterdays to help his tomorrows be a better version of himself, both physically and spiritually. This message impacts Todd profoundly. As he sits, staring at the ceiling of his office, he realizes the importance of everything that has happened to him. With his thoughts racing, Todd picks up the clean legal pad and begins to write. He is writing a letter to Tomorrow. He reflects on everything that he experienced today and feverishly writes his thoughts down so Tomorrow may read them and learn from him as a yesterday. The ideas begin to pour out of Todd's mind. It all makes perfect sense. This moment in his life is the ideal time for this message to come to the surface. He is facing a new decade of experience, his child will be born any day, and his career is about to take off.

As he pens the letter to Tomorrow, Todd realizes that this is the solution to the project he has been searching for. This message is something that he has to share with the world. *Just think of the people this can touch. Imagine the lives it can change,* Todd thinks, as his hand races across the paper. What feels like hours go by, as Todd scribbles across the pages of the legal pad. Turning page after page, he pours out his ideas and reflections. By writing the message, Todd is giving Tomorrow a playbook for the day ahead based on his experiences. As he writes his final thought, Todd places the legal pad back upon his desk. Leaning back in his chair, Todd takes a deep breath and runs his hand through his hair. The stress has left Todd's body, and he stands to take in the moment. Rising from the chair, Todd sees a person moving across the office. He recognizes the man's silhouette and begins calling out after him.

"Tomorrow, come here! You have to read this! Hey, man, come over here! I figured it all out!" Yelling excitedly after the sharply dressed man, Todd watches, as Tomorrow blindly passes him and turns down the corridor leading to the bathroom. Todd leaves his cubicle behind and jogs after Tomorrow, calling out his name. Turning the corner of the hallway, Todd watches Tomorrow push open the door and disappear into the bathroom. Seemingly a few steps behind him, Todd pursues Tomorrow through the door. Pushing it open, Todd is met with the blinding white light, yet again.

Procrastination is the bad habit of putting off until the day after tomorrow what should have been done the day before yesterday.
NAPOLEON HILL

CHAPTER SIX

PREPARING TOMORROW

The white light fades from his view, as Todd opens his eyes. There is a throbbing in his head, and his vision is blurred. Blinking rapidly, Todd begins to try to gather his surroundings. His face is cool on one side, and he can smell an overwhelming scent of bleach. As he moves his hands beneath his body, the surroundings start to become clearer. As he pushes himself to his feet, his vision clears, and Todd realizes that he is in the bathroom. Looking into the mirrored wall, where he saw Yesterday and the antique mirror, he sees his reflection alone staring back at him. His hair is a mess, his tie still unkempt around his untucked shirt, and there is a large, black-and-blue bruise on the right side of his head. As he stares into the mirror, it all becomes clear to Todd.

His game-winning shot resulted in a slip on the freshly mopped floor that sent him to the porcelain floor of the bathroom. *Was that all really a dream? It seemed so real,* Todd thinks to himself, as he rubs the swollen knot on his forehead. Looking down at his watch, Todd realizes that two hours have passed since he first entered the bathroom. In a panic, his thoughts immediately go to Grace waiting up for him. Breaking his gaze from the mirror, Todd makes his way to the door. Reaching out for the steel door handle, Todd freezes for a moment. He slowly opens the door, half-expecting the blinding white light. With the door creeping open, Todd peers around the frame and is met with the red hue of the exit sign from down the hall. Carefully stepping out of the doorway, Todd makes his way down the hallway.

The silence of the office is just how Todd left it. His desk lamp is the only bright light shining in the dimly lit room. Todd does not know what to expect, as he makes his way towards his desk. Although his experience was clearly a dream, everything felt so real, and he is filled with the revelations that came from it. Reaching his desk, Todd looks down in disappointment. The papers and reports are scattered all over the desktop, his pens are strewn about the entire area, and his cork board is covered with old memos and past-due emails.

Instinctively, Todd sits down and begins organizing his desk in the exact fashion it appeared to him in his dream. With each pen he places in the cup and with each report he stacks, Todd feels a sense of comfort and accomplishment. As he organizes the entire desktop, everything begins to appear as it did in his dream. Time passes by, and Todd cleans every square inch of his desk. Looking back up at the cork board, he smiles and lets out a laugh when he views all of the happy memories and the sonogram that brought him so much clarity in his dream. Placing the last paper upon the newly organized stack, Todd sits back in his chair and begins thinking to himself.

Well, there it is. I organized everything just as I saw it. Honestly, I feel great. I feel like I am on the path to becoming the best version of myself and preparing for tomorrow. With a newfound sense of accomplishment, Todd reaches into his desk drawer and pulls out a clean, fresh legal pad. He places it in the exact spot that he saw in his dream, and, with that, he places the final touch on his newly organized desk. Everything came together for Todd. He truly feels that he began using his yesterdays to better his tomorrow. Having finished his organizing, Todd rises from his chair, grabs his suit jacket and keys, and shuts off his desk lamp. Making his way through the empty office to the exit, Todd stops and looks at the bathroom door. Thinking to himself, Todd reflects yet again, *Who would have known that all this would come from a trip to the bathroom? I guess I was right when I told myself that we would take one trip to the bathroom, come back, and knock this thing out of the park. I just hope I didn't get a concussion from all of this.* Laughing at himself, Todd walks past the bathroom door and makes his way down to the parking garage.

The drive home is filled with silence. Todd's mind is exhausted, and his head is still throbbing. The experience that he had throughout his dream is really impacting him. He knows that this yesterday will certainly be one he will remember for quite some time. Returning to the dark road after stopping at the store to get Grace her ice cream, Todd thinks to himself, again, *I can't believe I am going to be a father. What an awesome experience this is all going to be. I'm sure it will be challenging at times, but if I just keep using my yesterdays, I know I will always bring a better tomorrow into that little guy's life.* As he continues down the dark road, Todd's mind drifts, and he begins to make practical sense of what he just experienced.

Sitting in the silence of his car, Todd's mind begins running at a hundred miles an hour again. *So how does all of this work? When do we cross over from today to yesterday? Am I in today? Is everything that happened yesterday? How does today become yesterday and tomorrow become today?* Todd is unbelievably confused. Throughout the entire message from Yesterday, he never actually tried to make a practical set of guidelines to follow. He looked at the situation from the big picture and never attempted to break down the smaller pieces of the message in order to use it. If he cannot identify when his todays became yesterdays, then there is no way that he can use them effectively. Furthermore, Todd realizes that if he waited until tomorrow to reflect on his yesterday, then he is already behind the ball and is losing precious time in the tomorrow that became his new today. In the silence of his car on the dark road, Todd refocuses his mind and begins to break down the message he received.

Okay, Todd, just think. You're the idea guy. You can make sense of this. The breakdown is simple. Today's yesterday stays a yesterday. That part is simple. Once you reach yesterday, that is where you stay. So everything that has happened today up until this very moment has moved from being a today to a yesterday. As we move throughout our today, we are building the yesterday that can be used to fuel the tomorrow. Working through this problem makes Todd feel as if he is making sense of the things that were racing through his mind. His thoughts continue, as he shifts his focus.

Okay, so yesterday is figured out, Todd thinks to himself, as everything begins to become clearer to him. *That means that today is really just a junction for yesterday and tomorrow. It is the place where we have the ability to act. Since yesterday is set in stone and tomorrow is an unknown, today is our opportunity to act. Today is really just a series of small moments that come and go very quickly. That means that today is the vehicle for us to use the process. Yeah, that makes sense.* The road ahead begins to turn. He can see the familiar sight of his neighborhood. Continuing his journey home, Todd shifts his thoughts yet again.

So if yesterday is set in stone and is what we use to reflect on, then it is the motive for our actions, which are found in our todays. That means that our tomorrows need to be the result of whatever our actions are. They are the desired outcomes that we have established from reflecting on our yesterdays and acting in our todays. So, simply put, yesterday is our motive to act. It is the groundwork that we use to create a game plan for our todays and tomorrows. Our todays are the actual actions that we use to accomplish that plan, and our tomorrow is the end product of all our motives and actions. By reflecting on yesterday and acting in today, we are building for a more effective and productive tomorrow. Todd feels extremely accomplished having reached this conclusion. It all begins to make sense to him in a much more detailed way. However, Todd is still unclear on how to begin the process.

So now that I know the way this system is supposed to work, how does it start? When does today become yesterday and we start building for tomorrow? Todd freezes, stopping the car in the middle of the road, as everything becomes clear to him. *Wait a minute! I got it! There is a starting point for everyone to start using their yesterdays to better their tomorrows. What you have to do is live a full today, acting and going through the motions of life. At the conclusion of that day, you have to sit down and plan for the day that is coming. Reflecting on that today, which has now become a yesterday, you are setting yourself up to live the fullest tomorrow you can.*

Todd finally figured it out. This monumental moment for him is the starting point of a new way of life. He will use today as his starting point and recap everything he experienced, the same way he did on the legal pad in his dream. He will take his today, which now began the transformation into a yesterday, to be the motive for his tomorrow so he knows how to act when that tomorrow becomes a today. All this is so clear to Todd now. He puts the car back into drive and continues down the dark road, feeling enlightened and a sense of happiness he never felt.

Turning onto his street, Todd can see the driveway light beaming from his house. Grace always left the lights on for Todd when he came home. This simple gesture makes him smile at first, but it then brings him back to a place of reflection. Todd realizes that he does not want Grace to be responsible for leaving the lights on so much. He is always coming home late and making her go throughout the house turning lights on so he can see. As he pulls into the driveway, Todd stays in his running car and looks upon the house. His mind is filled with reflection, and he reaches a moment of disappointment.

Thinking to himself, Todd expresses his thoughts, *Gosh, Grace really is something else. She never forgets to leave the lights on. She is always concerned about me and my well-being. She really is the glue that holds us together. How has she put up with me this long? I am not going to make her have to leave the lights on anymore. I am going to come home and help her with these new things on the horizon. I am not going to use my yesterdays as a half-committed husband and allow them to fuel my tomorrows. I am going to use those yesterdays to make me a fully committed and more caring husband tomorrow.* Todd finishes and realizes it is time he makes his way into the house.

Stepping out of his car and walking up the lit driveway, Todd feels a sense of relief and comfort in returning home. He truly believes that this is the start of a new version of himself. This day is going to become the most influential yesterday he has ever had. Reaching for the door knob, Todd smiles and is thankful to be met with the dim light of his house and not a blinding white sensation.

Yesterday is gone. Tomorrow has yet to come.
We have only today. Let us begin.
MOTHER TERESA

CHAPTER SEVEN

COMING HOME

Walking through the side door of his house, Todd passes through his home office. Noticing the mess that his desk has become, he stops and thinks that needs to be addressed. However, at the moment, the pressing issue is putting his tired mind to rest and seeing his beautiful wife. Making his way into the large, open-concept kitchen-and-living room, Todd smiles after seeing that the side-table lamp was left on for him. Grace started leaving the lights on in the house because Todd is notorious for running into the island in the kitchen or the side tables along the couch, when he comes home late. She is always looking out for Todd. Grace is truly the organizer and the planner. Without her, Todd realizes that he will be totally lost; his entire life will look like his desk before he placed it in order. She is the balance in his life, and he is truly thankful for her.

Creeping through the house, he sets his keys on the

kitchen island and moves towards their bedroom door. Slowly opening the door, Todd is startled to see the bedroom lights on and his wife sitting up in bed. "Hi, babe." Todd says. "Is everything okay? Why are you still awake? It's almost three in the morning." He speaks in a concerned tone.

"I'm fine, Todd" Grace says. "I'm just pregnant. The heartburn was killing me, and I got sick lying down, so I decided to sit up. I swear this son of yours better not be getting comfortable in there. He is supposed to be out of me any day now, and I don't know if I can handle this anymore." Grace is clearly distraught and in pain.

"Oh, geez." Todd says. "I'm sorry, babe. Is there anything I can do for you? Want me to rub your feet?" At the same time as he speaks, he leans over and kisses Grace on the forehead. Todd's mind is finally at peace, and he feels normal for the first time all night. Grace's presence in his life is truly the most calming thing he has.

"No, my feet are fine, but what happened to your head, Todd?" Grace asks. "That bruise is terrible! Oh, my God, it's huge!" At the same time as she speaks, she runs her hands over the bruise on Todd's forehead. Todd completely forgot about the golfball-sized welt that was coming off his forehead. He does not want to tell Grace the entire story and bother her with everything that was going on. Up to this point, he has been lying to Grace about the project, and she believes that he has everything under control. Todd freezes, as her hand leaves his forehead and comes to rest on his shoulder. He knows that it is time to let her in on the truth and the experience that he had.

"Oh, this old thing?" Todd says, while smirking and running his hand through his hair. "I hit my head in the bath-room tonight at work. It really was quite the blow."

"Do you want me to get you some ice or something?" Grace asks. "That thing is really nasty, Todd." She is clearly more concerned about the bruise than Todd is.

"I'm just fine, babe. Thank you, though. Why don't I go make you a bowl of ice cream? I have something pretty important that I want to tell you." Todd rises from the bedside, as Grace nods, clearly still concerned about the condition of Todd's game-winning injury. Walking into the kitchen, Todd opens the freezer, and the cool air washes over his face. He knows that he has to tell Grace about the message that he received, but he can probably spare her the details of his wild dream. This is Todd's first chance to explain the message to someone else. He decides that he will give Grace the most practical version that he can come up with. By doing this, Todd believes that she will not get lost in the maze that is his thoughts. Todd becomes excited, as he walks back into the bedroom with a bowl of ice cream.

Handing the bowl to his wife, Todd sits down on the bed next to her. "Okay, babe, I want to start off by telling you the truth. I totally put this project off to the last minute. I had ignored it and ignored it from the very start. I'm glad I got that off my chest." As Todd continues to speak, Grace interrupts him.

"Todd, did you really think I didn't know that?" Grace says. "You always do that sort of thing. It's just the way you are. I just really hope that something changes inside of you so you don't teach our son that way of life," At the same time as she speaks, she scoops another spoonful of ice cream into her mouth. Hearing Grace actually say those words to him face-to-face has a large impact on Todd. The excitement that he possessed when he walked into the bedroom is replaced with sadness. He feels truly awful for having put Grace through living with him, neglecting his yesterdays, and, more so, he feels terrible that she is now worried he will teach his son the same way of life. Pulling himself together, Todd answers his wife.

"I know, Grace. I am really sorry about that. Not just about this project, but also about the man I have been over our entire relationship." As Todd finishes speaking, his shoulders lower and depression is clearly over his face.

"It's okay, Todd," Grace answers, while swallowing her spoonful of ice cream. "Really, it is. Thank you for that, though. Whatever it is that you feel guilty about, just remember it's in the past and all we can do is move forward. So why don't you tell me about this project? I am sensing something different about you." Hearing his wife's caring response restores the excitement that Todd had when he first walked into the room. With his spirits lifted, Todd shifts his weight and sits up straight, next to his pregnant wife.

"Well, it just so happens that I believe I have the whole project figured out. I just hope it makes sense to you and to other people. So, basically, life is divided up into three categories: yesterdays, todays, and tomorrows. It starts with using our yesterdays and reflecting on them. You have to look back at where you have been and see the good and the bad that has come from your yesterdays. This allows you to have a clearer picture of how you have gotten to where you are. The important thing is to take care of your yesterdays and to use them as your motives for your todays. Following me so far?" Grace nods, and Todd hopes that he is making sense.

"Too many of us allow the burdens from yesterday to impact our tomorrows," Todd says. "The things that we chose not to do, or the feelings and the actions we perform, can all hinder or help our tomorrow. See, our yesterdays are set in stone. Once the day is over, that yesterday is never changing. It is just how we use them that matters. Our todays are where we act. We have to use our yesterdays inside our todays to create a better tomorrow. Because our tomorrows are an unknown, we have to use the motive of yesterday to power our actions of today. Basically, we have to use our past to give us a clear picture of our present to ensure a better future."

"Does all this make any sense?" Todd asks his wife, hoping that she is following.

"Yeah, it does actually. That is a really insightful message," Grace says, as she scoops another mound of ice cream into her mouth.

"I am so happy that you understand this," Todd says. "I was really worried that none of it was going to make sense. Well, in a nutshell, that is what I am going to use for the project." He speaks with a sense of pride filling his voice.

"Todd," Grace says, with a puzzled look on her face. "Umm, I think that it is a great message, but how are you going to take that approach to life and apply it in a practical way that people can use to better their lives?" Todd's stomach drops. He never thought about that. He was so excited about the revelation he received that he did not realize that there is no way for people to actually use his message. Through all of that, he never actually created a product that allows people to use the message.

"Grace, you are completely right," Todd says. "How did I not see this sooner? All I did was come up with the foundation for something. I still have the whole house to build." At the same time as he speaks, he lies back and stares at his bedroom ceiling. Lost in thought, Todd closes his eyes and begins to replay the dream in his mind, searching for the answer. As he found himself sitting in the coffee shop, speaking to Yesterday, he saw the Journal of Yesterdays sitting on the white tablecloth. As Todd envisions this scene, he quickly sits up and grabs his wife by the shoulders.

"That's it! I got it, babe!" Todd says. "I know what the answer is! It's the Journal of Yesterdays! How did I not see this sooner!?" He appears almost in a state of madness, as he looks at his wife, with a huge smile on his face.

"What is the Journal of Yesterdays?" Grace asks, clearly confused at Todd's current state. Todd lets go of his wife's shoulders and regains his composure, realizing he has to explain this to his wife.

"Oh, right," Todd says. "I'm sorry. It's essentially a journal that you keep about all of your days. It lets you go back and see your yesterdays as a story and use them to help guide the actions of your today to get to your tomorrow. It's almost like a recap of your day as a today and also a letter to your upcoming tomorrow." At the same time as he speaks, he eagerly grins at his wife, hoping this is the idea. Grace puts her finger on the corner of her mouth and begins to think.

"Well, I think that's a good starting point, but I see one big problem, in that I would never be able to use it," Grace says affirmatively. Todd feels his stomach drop again. He really believes that the Journal of Yesterdays was the answer to his project. Clearly feeling defeated, Todd listens, as his wife continues.

"We need something that lets us use the message, reflect a little each day, maybe have a big reflection each week, and give us a way to prioritize our life," Grace says. "Not everyone can get into deep thought the way you can, Todd. Actually, a lot of people just want something that will help them live better and be more efficient in their todays and tomorrows. Maybe you should combine the journal with a planner. You know, like each day gets two pages. On one day, you have your goals, schedule, and things you don't want to forget for that day. Then, the other page is a summary of your day and a space to write your thoughts for tomorrow. That way, each day you aren't overwhelmed with the burden of having to think so much. It is kind of laid out for you already. Then, at the end of each week, you can have a big reflection, maybe like a guided writing prompt or something. It would just be easier to have to think deeply only once a week and let the other todays be organized and more efficient. You still get to use your yesterdays. You just aren't overburdening people with having to think as much. You don't want it to be something you think about. You want this to be the way people start living. Does this make sense?" At the same time as she speaks, she looks at Todd with tired eyes.

"Oh my gosh, Grace," Todd says. "You are a genius! That is incredible! I would have never thought of that! This is the project. That is a million-dollar idea. There is just so much that can come from that. You are totally right. It isn't something I want people to have to think about each day.

It should just become your way of life. Gosh, you really are something else, beautiful!" So Todd finishes, kissing his wife passionately. Grace pushes Todd off her and starts laughing, as she wipes the sloppy kiss from her mouth.

"I am glad I could help," Grace says. "Now, I am really pregnant, and that was my birthday gift to you. So I am going to try and get some sleep. You should, too, birthday boy. Who knows? Maybe your son will have a present for you, too." At the same time as she speaks, she lowers herself into the bed and shuts her eyes.

"I love you, babe. You truly are amazing. I am one lucky guy," Todd says, as he brushes the hair from Grace's face.

"I love you too, Todd. Now let this pregnant woman get some sleep." As Grace fades off to sleep, Todd sits and watches her breathe. She is so beautiful in all of her pregnant glory. He feels truly as if he is the luckiest man on Earth. Slowly rising from the bed, Todd creeps to his office. Sitting down in front of his computer, Todd pushes all the mess out of his way and begins to feverishly work on creating a prototype of the "Every Yesterday Journal."

*We usually lose today because there has
been a yesterday, and tomorrow is coming.*
JOHANN WOLFGANG VON GOETHE

CHAPTER EIGHT

BOARD MEETING

"We didn't start the fire, it was always burnin' since the world was turnin', we didn't start the fire, no, we didn't light it!!!" The blaring Billy Joel echoes through the house as Todd scrambles to shut off his alarm clock. Locating his phone, Todd realizes that he never made it to his bed. He fell asleep on the keyboard at his desk. Rubbing his eyes, he looks back at his phone and realizes that he has only slept for three hours. Slowly making his way back through the dark house, Todd stops and looks at his beautiful wife sleeping. Quietly navigating his bedroom, he turns on the shower and steps inside. With the warm water running over his face, Todd thinks about the things that this day may contain. Today is the day that his career is either defined or over. Everything depends on the "Every Yesterday" project. This is officially the make-it-or-break-it moment of his professional life.

Moving closer to the showerhead, Todd begins to think about the possibility of the board members rejecting his idea. His mind races as he thinks about the disappointment for Grace, the idea of bringing his son into the world without having a job, and the struggle of trying to find a new one. As he shuts off the water, Todd steps in front of his bathroom mirror. Bracing himself on the sink, he looks at his reflection and finds himself in a very familiar place. He realizes that he was spending a lot of time looking into mirrors lately. Speaking quietly, Todd addresses the negative thoughts filling his mind.

"Okay, champ, listen here. This is all going to work out. Just like Yesterday said in the dream, you know this message is something that can work. Just think about what it has done for you in the short time you have had it. We are going to walk in there and knock this thing out of the park." Todd finishes his motivational speech and walks himself into the closet.

Looking at his rack of suits, Todd finds just the right one. It is the suit that Grace bought him for his first day of work. He pulls the suit off the rack and begins to dress in the same attire that he saw Tomorrow wearing during his dream. Everything, down to the cuff links, is exactly as Todd remembered. Putting the finishing touches on his slick-backed hair, Todd makes his way back into the bedroom. Creeping closer to Grace's side of the bed, Todd leans down and whispers in her ear, "I love you, babe. I am going to go kick this day's butt and make for us an even better tomorrow."

"I love you, Todd. I know you are going to do great. Happy birthday, my love," Grace says, as she rolls back over and falls into a deep sleep. Todd makes his way out to the driveway and gets in his car to make the drive into the office. The streets are empty this early in the morning. It is really a peaceful experience. Leaving the radio off, Todd seems to make every green light at the intersections on the way to the office.

Man, maybe this really is my day! I never make those lights! Todd thinks, as he pulls into the parking garage. For the first time in over five years, Todd is able to park in the first row of parking spots. This is a small victory for him, largely because he hates walking from the last row. Making his way out of the parking garage and onto the street in front of his office building, Todd looks out at the horizon and sees the sun begin to peek into the dark sky.

This is something he never took the time to embrace. The rising sun means a lot to Todd on this day. This is the today that he is going to start using his yesterdays, and, with that rising sun, he is a new man rising from his experiences. He grabs the brass knob on the door of the coffee shop and hears the familiar tone of the meditation bells hanging above. His eyes immediately focus on the table that he and Yesterday sat at in his dream. It all does seem so real to Todd. Stepping to the counter, Todd orders a black coffee and a granola bar, just as he saw Tomorrow do in his dream. Paying the cashier, Todd takes a long sip of coffee and starts his way back to his office.

Arriving at his office, Todd stops at his cubicle and sees the beautifully organized desk. He is filled with the same sense of accomplishment from the night before. Gathering his supplies and printing off the prototype from his email, Todd moves into the unoccupied conference room to prepare for the presentation. Todd works tirelessly, putting the finishing touches on the message that he hoped would propel his career forward.

After placing the finishing touches on his presentation, Todd looks up from the podium, as the board members begin filing into the conference room. Todd greets them and hands out copies of the proposal to each member of the board. As the board members exchange pleasantries, Todd assumes his position at the front of the room. He is staring at the long, oval table filled with the men and women who will decide his future. As the small talk subsides, Todd positions his notes and begins to speak.

"Good morning, ladies and gentleman. The first thing I would like to say is thank you for trusting me with this opportunity and for giving me the chance to work on such a monumental project for our company. I understand that many of you believe that, in order to keep up with the competing companies, we should abandon our printing services completely. While the digital age is most certainly upon us, I believe that this idea could very well be the biggest thing our company has ever produced. What I ask from you during this presentation is that you keep an open mind and truly think about yourselves, as we move through this journey together." He reads the facial expressions of the board members and casually runs his hand through his freshly slicked-back hair. The board members vary in range—from those completely skeptical and disinterested to those mildly amused and intrigued—that he is going to keep print media going. They do, however, all seem to raise an eyebrow at his suggestion to keep an open mind, so maybe there is a glimmer of hope, after all. Todd knows he is fighting an uphill battle. Ignoring the drop in his stomach, Todd takes a deep breath and begins to speak again.

"This presentation is about a product that is not just a gimmick or something that I believe will sell. It is about a product that encourages a philosophy of life that will drastically improve the happiness and productivity of all those who choose to embark on it. In the short time of using this product, it has dramatically changed not just my personal outlook on the world but also my personality. We all reach large moments of reflection in our lives. With my birthday here today, my son soon to be on the way, and the importance of this project, I reevaluated the approach I had as a person. The result was this message. So, by a show of hands, how many of us in this room, at one time or another, have put something off until the next day or left something to the last minute?" He then walks around the room. Slowly, all the board members raise their hands in the air.

"Okay, thank you. You can put your hands down. Procrastination is something that plagues every single working professional. From the very top of an organization and all the way to the bottom, human nature is to take advantage of the tomorrow that we have and place the burdens of today onto it. What this product does is create an effective way to live your lives in order to avoid procrastinating not only with the physical actions of our lives but also in our personal lives. Procrastination is not something that lives only in the physical actions of our lives. Many of us procrastinate becoming the best version of ourselves, as well, because, in large part, of being consumed by our daily lives. See, that is the truly beautiful thing about this message. By using the experiences of our yesterdays to fuel a better tomorrow, we find ourselves free from the burdens of daily life, which allows us to spend a little more time focusing on ourselves as people." Todd finishes making his point and notices a change in the board members. The skeptical members put their phones down and began to focus on Todd with much greater intensity. Seeing his opportunity, Todd decides that this is his moment to drive home the big point.

"When you break down our lives, it is fairly easy. There are three categories in which we can break down our days spent in this life. The first is the easiest to understand; that's our yesterdays. Yesterdays are the days that are behind us. It is all of our days and the moments that we have lived through. Once moments in our lives reach yesterday, that's where they stay. How we use them is the real question at hand. The next part of life is our today. This is the moment that we live in each day. Today is the moment in our life that we can act. It is the only part of life that we can change what is happening to us. These actions are what make up our journey. The last phase of our life journey is tomorrow. This is the unknown part of the system. None of us know what tomorrow has in store for us, but wouldn't it be great if we had a system that assured we took care of everything we could to ensure it would be a great day? That's where all of this comes together."

Todd pauses, realizing that the entire room is captivated by his message. It is time for him to deliver the big, home run point. This is it right here. He has truly reached the breaking point of this entire journey. Taking a sip from his water bottle, Todd moves back to the front of the room and stands at the head of the table.

"With that understanding, let's bring it all together. We

need to be able to reflect on our yesterdays and use them as the motive for our actions in our today, which hopefully bring the desired result of our tomorrows. Instead of taking our yesterdays for granted and not using them as motivation to act in our todays, we need to seize the experience that we all have and restructure the way we live. The days of putting off the burdens of our yesterdays onto our tomorrows are over. As a company, we are going to inspire people to seize the moment of their todays in pursuit of a better tomorrow. This is not just an inspirational message. It is a system that will truly lead to a better and more effective life for our customers, both physically and spiritually. With that said, if you wouldn't mind turning your proposal to the last page. What you are looking at is the prototype of the way we are going to change people's lives. Those two pages hold the 'Yesterday Journal.' It is a yearly based journal that allows us to keep our days in order and reflect on where we are in this world. It allows us to keep track of our yesterdays, recount our actions of the today, and write letters to our tomorrows. By doing all of that, we can self-reflect on our weeks as a whole and, ultimately, get ourselves using our yesterdays to their fullest potential. That way, we start creating effective and strategic actions in our todays based on those motives. Ultimately, this all brings a better, more positive result-orientated approach to our tomorrows. The real question, ladies and gentleman, is are you ready to become the best version of yourself? If you are, let's get this message out there and create a world where people break free from the procrastination of life and start living the Every Yesterday Life." Todd finishes his presentation and braces himself on the tabletop.

The board members are all perched on the ends of their seats. It is clear that they are fully engaged in Todd's message. Todd is filled with anticipation at what the members are thinking. Sweat begins to trickle down his forehead, and a knot is forming in his stomach. Just as Todd begins to feel light-headed from his nerves, Mr. Auerbach, the company's president, rises from his seat. "Okay, Todd, if you wouldn't mind stepping outside to give us a moment to discuss your presentation, we will reach a conclusion." Todd steps outside of the conference room and sits at his desk. Staring at his cork board, he looks at Grace's smiling face and the sonogram of his son. His stomach is in knots, and sweat begins to pour from his forehead. *This was it. Everything I have ever worked for is in the hands of those people in that board room*, Todd thinks to himself, as he fiddles with his stapler, trying to keep his mind busy. This is easily the most stressful moment of Todd's life. He never put so much effort and belief in a project before. He truly feels this is his life's work. Dropping the stapler on the ground, Todd bends beneath his desk and tells himself to regain his composure. Fumbling amongst the computer wires in search of the stapler, Todd hears Mr. Auerbach yelling into the office.

"Yester! Where are you? We are ready for you in here." Emerging from beneath the desk like a gopher from his hole, Todd hurries to his feet and powerwalks back into the conference room. Taking a seat at the head of the table, Todd prepares himself for the worst, as Mr. Auerbach positions himself in his chair and begins to speak.

"Yester, that was the most inspirational and innovative presentation I have heard in quite some time. You, sir, have knocked this today out of the park. This idea is something that I need very much in my life, and I know everyone at this table feels the same. I look forward to moving this to the next stage of production. You will be moving to the third floor and assuming the role of production supervisor over this project. Congratulations, Mr. Yester; we all look forward to seeing the results from all of the tomorrows that come with this project."

Todd freezes. Filled with excitement, he is at a loss for words. Regaining his composure, Todd answers Mr. Auerbach, "Yes sir, thank you for believing in me. I promise you this project will get the best version of myself, and the tomorrows that are to follow will be exactly what we are all anticipating." The board members rise, and all line up to begin shaking Todd's hand, while asking him questions about his message. It is clear this is something that they all feel very strongly about. As Todd answers the questions from the engaging board members, his conversation is interrupted by the ringing of his cell phone.

Make it so today is not like yesterday and tomorrow will be different FOREVER.
Tony Robbins

CHAPTER NINE

FADING INTO YESTERDAY

Pressing the silent button on his phone, Todd continues the conversations. As he listens to the praise of the board members, his phone begins ringing again. Excusing himself from the conversation, Todd steps from the conference room and looks down at his phone. Grace's number runs across the screen, and Todd panics the way an expecting father does around the due date of his child.

"Hi, babe. Is everything okay?" Todd asks, half-expecting his wife to scream in pain on the other end of the phone. In a calm, collected tone, Grace answers her concerned husband.

"Yeah, honey, everything is fine. How did your presentation go?" Todd's stomach returns to normal, and he regains his composure.

"It went great!" Todd says. "They promoted me to production supervisor and are going to run the project into production! I couldn't ask for more! It truly has been an amazing day, but being able to share this with you has been the best part. I can't wait to get home and celebrate! This is the best birthday ever!" He is hoping Grace can hear the smile that is on his face through his voice.

"That awesome, babe!" Grace says. "I knew you would do great. This really has been an amazing day so far! Definitely one we will never forget. By the way, I am on my way to the hospital with your mom. Your son wants to be a birthday present." Grace speaks in a calm, collected tone. Todd's stomach drops, his heart begins to race, and his mind starts spinning out of control.

"WHAT! Ummm, okay, I am on my way! I'll be there as fast as I can! Jeez, okay, I am coming," Todd frantically yells into the phone, beginning to pace, while thinking about what his next move should be. In a calming tone, Grace answers her ridiculous husband.

"Todd, everything is fine. Take your time and get here safe. I promise that everything is just fine. I love you and I'll see you soon." As she finishes, Todd is left speechless and scrambling for his car keys.

"Okay, okay, deep breath. I am going to meet you there. I love you, babe." Hanging up the phone, Todd turns back to the board members and realizes they had just watched him run around the office like a mad man during the duration of the phone call. The board members are looking at him as if they fully regret their decision of running with the project and that they may need to call the police. Mr. Auerbach looks at Todd and speaks in a concerned tone.

"Yester, is everything okay?" the president asks, as he shows a clear sense of dismay with Todd's actions. Todd does not care at all what the board members think at this moment. He is about to become a father and is entitled to look like a complete moron.

"Yes sir! Everything is great! I am about to become a father! We are going to have to pick this up tomorrow. My wife is on the way to the hospital! I am going to be a dad! My son is coming!" Todd yells at the top of his lungs and runs towards the exit. The board members all clap their hands and wish Todd well, as he disappears towards the stairwell. Emerging into the parking garage, Todd begins sprinting towards the last row of cars. Realizing about halfway there that he parked in the first row, he retraces his steps and is sure he looks like an idiot yet again. As he climbs into the driver seat of his car, Todd's heart is racing, and he is breathing heavily. It is a short, ten-minute drive to the hospital. He prays for his luck with the green lights to continue.

Driving on the crowded roads, Todd slams on his horn and acts like a man possessed. He is consumed with nothing but the thought of his pregnant wife being alone. Barreling his way through traffic, Todd begins to calm himself down. He realizes that he will do Grace no good, all worked up like this, and that he needs to remain calm and collected for her. As he continues to catch the green lights down main street, Todd pulls into the hospital parking lot and runs inside in a full sprint. Having no idea where to go, Todd frantically finds an information desk.

"My wife….baby…..where…do….I…..go?" Todd says, breathing so heavily he can't even get the words out. The young receptionist chuckles. She is clearly used to the crazed fathers-to-be.

"Go right down that hallway, sir. I am pretty sure your

wife was just rolled into Room 22. Good luck." Todd waves his hand frantically at her and thanks her for the directions. Coming to a sliding stop in the doorway of Room 22, Todd attempts to take a deep breath so Grace will not be able to tell that he was sprinting.

"Grace, are you in here?" Todd asks. Letting out a huge breath, he realizes that trying to hide that he was sprinting was a futile effort. He walks into the room and sees the nurses and their doctor crowded around his beautiful wife. She is sweating and clearly in pain. She clutches his hand and lets out a groaning comment.

"I love you, honey. Happy birthday, but I swear to God, don't ever ask me for another one of these," she says, gripping Todd's hand more and more tightly with each word. Having the baby around this time was Grace's idea, but Todd decides this is not the best time to remind her of that. Todd is instructed to change into the scrubs outfit and follows the birthing team into the delivery room. Everything goes perfectly. Thomas Todd Yester is born on his father's birthday at 12:36 p.m. He is a healthy baby boy. Todd is left filled with a sense of pride and love he never experienced before. As he sits in the rocking chair beside his wife, holding his son, Todd cannot help letting a tear roll down his face.

"Grace, this is the most beautiful day of my life. You did great in there. I am so proud of you. I love you with all my heart," Todd says, as he reaches out and caresses his wife's arm. Her skin is still flushed from the strain of the delivery. Grace tickles Thomas's stomach and looks at Todd.

"I love you, Todd. This really is something else. Can you please put Thomas in his bassinet? I am going to try and get some sleep." Todd takes his son from his wife's arms. Holding the small child in his arms, Todd begins to speak softly, as he walks towards the bassinet.

"Hey there, buddy. I'm your dad. I am sure one day you are going to figure that out. Just so you know, you have made this day the best birthday—and yesterday—I could ever have. I am going to give you the best tomorrows you could ever wish for. We can save that conversation for your baby's first 'Every Yesterday' journal in a few years. There ya go; nice and soft for the little man." He places his son in the bassinet.

Returning to his chair, Todd begins to reflect on the days he experienced. He became Tomorrow from his dream and lived through all of the today that was in store for him. Todd can feel his brain drifting into the reflection of today, as it begins to turn into a yesterday. As he looks at the bassinet holding his son, it suddenly dawns on him that all three of his parts of life are with him in every moment. At any moment, we are a combination of our yesterdays, our today, and our tomorrow. All three feed off one another. Todd sits back in the chair and reaches for his work bag, as his wife and son sleep peacefully. Pulling the legal pad from his desk out of the bag, Todd begins to flip for a clean page. To his astonishment, he sees the letter that he wrote to his tomorrow in his dream. *How was this possible?* Todd thinks to himself. *Had some of that actually happened?* His mind races, as he begins to read the letter he penned himself.

Dear Tomorrow,

You have this place in tip-top shape. I mean, the desk is perfect. I am not too sure how I got here and what all of this means. I think some of it is starting to become clear to me. I want you to know exactly what it is that I am thinking at this moment. I have spent the entire night living through my yesterdays and the failures that were a part of my life up until this point. I realize that I have been totally taking advantage of the experiences that we have lived through. Each day I push the burdens from yesterday onto today, which hinders our tomorrows. I am sure this will all make more sense by the time you read this. For now, I just don't want you to have to feel the way I do about my yesterdays when you become our today. I want you to be proud of the man you were yesterday. I want the day that you live as a today to be set up by me as your yesterday. I just want to start making a difference in my life and my wife's life and to set up my tomorrows for my son. I am tired of being some of the people who take their yesterdays for granted and who take advantage of their tomorrows. From here on out, I am going to live by a simple motto: "What are you going to do today to make this day a yesterday you will be proud of tomorrow?" Good luck, buddy.

Sincerely,

Todd

Rereading the note, Todd remembers writing that motto at the bottom of the letter. That is truly the entire point of this whole message. Todd realizes that this statement encompasses how all three phases live within one moment. Staring at the legal pad, Todd swears to never forget that motto. He feels a strong sense of closure after reading his note from yesterday. Todd is completely unclear on how this note surfaced in the legal pad that he swore was blank.

As he thumbs through the other pages, all of his notes about the message are written in his classic chicken scratch and multicolored inks. This is amazing, and Todd is left speechless. As he places the pad on his lap, Todd's eyes are met with darkness.

"Todd, wake up. Honey, wake up and come take a picture with your son." Todd can hear Grace's voice. He opens his eyes and realizes that he dreamt the entire scene about finding his note from yesterday. Chuckling to himself, Todd decides he should really pay greater attention to his dreams. He steps over to his wife's bedside and looks at his mother, who is waiting with her iPhone to take a picture. After snapping the picture, Todd's mother steps over to him and gives him a big hug.

This moment is truly perfect in Todd's mind. Everything worked out just the way he hoped. The beautiful day is fading into yesterday, and Todd cannot wait to see what his tomorrow will bring. He does not know what it will hold. However, he does know that he can look back on these yesterdays and be proud of them tomorrow.

Jesus Christ is the same yesterday, today, and forever.
HEBREWS 13:8

CHAPTER TEN

ONE YEAR LATER

The open-concept kitchen-and-living room is filled with all of Todd's closest friends and family. Everyone came together to celebrate Thomas's first birthday. It is truly amazing to Todd, who is looking out at all of the people filling his house. This child is loved by so many people. The whole experience is truly amazing. Todd watches, as his son waddles around the home, from person to person. Thomas grew so much over the first year of his life. Todd is filled with pride and joy, as he watches his beautiful wife chase the one-year-old around the house and scoop him up into her arms.

Everyone in the home gathers around the dining room table, as Thomas sits in his high chair. Todd bought a cake, with the picture from the day Thomas was born printed on it. Grace lights the candle, and the room erupts in a heart-felt version of "Happy Birthday." Watching his young son jam his hands into the cake and smear the icing all over himself, Todd can't help smiling. Holding tears back from his eyes, Todd walks behind his son, as his mother positions herself to take a picture of his family over the cake. This is truly a beautiful moment in Todd's life. He moves to the kitchen and reflects over the scene that was his home. *Gosh, this truly has been one heck of a year. I could have never dreamed what those tomorrows would bring. Thank you, Yesterday. You have shown me so much. Without you, I would have never gotten to this beautiful today.* As Todd paces across his kitchen, his brother-in-law, Gary, playfully punches him in the arm.

"My favorite brother, Todd, the big important board member. Let's step outside so you can tell me more about this stuff my sister has been telling me." Todd follows Gary out to the front porch of his house. Sitting down in the two wooden Adirondack chairs, Todd begins to speak.

"All right, Gary, what is it that you want to know?" Todd askes his clearly eager brother-in-law.

"Ya know, man," Gary says. "Tell me the story. I saw you right before this time last year. You were working in a cubicle, and I was starting to worry about my sister's choice in a husband. Now, I hear you are a board member at the company and the brand supervisor for some new product. Frankly, my man, I didn't think you had this in you. What changed? I have to know!" As he speaks, he leans to the edge of the wooden Adirondack chair.

"Yeah, I guess that is true," Todd says. "The last time you saw me, I was quite the mess. This year really has been a crazy ride. Thomas was born, I launched the Every Yesterday brand, became a board member at the company, and have really created an awesome marriage with Grace. Every Yesterday is what changed my life. The company has taken the idea, and, together, we have built it into a brand. We have an Every Yesterday version for all types of people: college students, mothers-to-be, marriages, high school students, and parents. The message has really taken on a life of its own." He beams with pride over what he has accomplished.

"That's what I am talking about, man!" Gary says. "I need to know what this Every Yesterday thing is all about! If it can do all that for you, I am sure it can do something for me. Do you mind sharing with me?" He moves so far up on the chair he is almost standing.

"I don't mind at all. I guess the best place to start is with Yesterday. Buckle up, Gary. This story is quite the ride. It all started when I hit this game-winning shot…"